I'm a NICU STRONG baby!

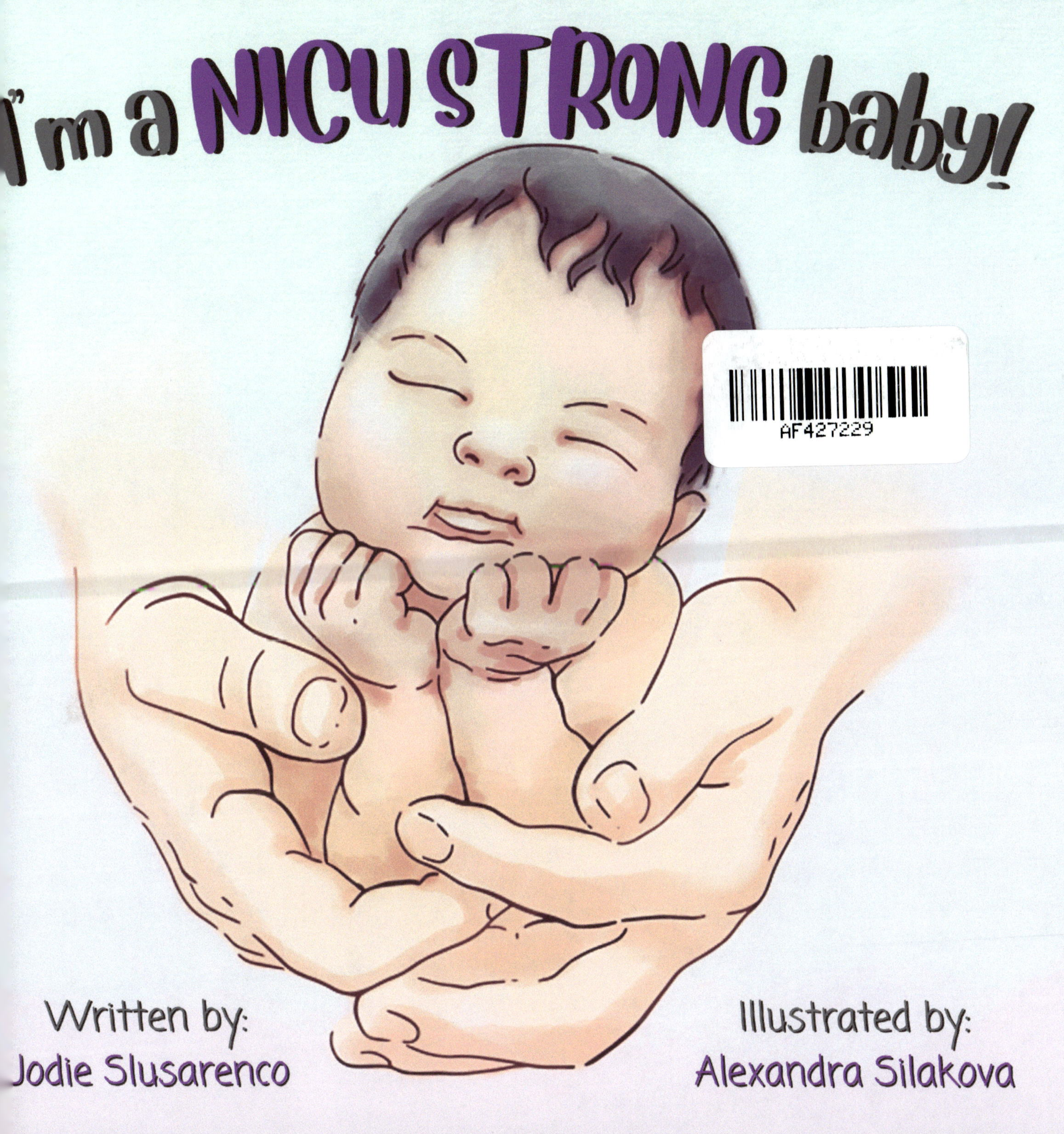

Written by:
Jodie Slusarenco

Illustrated by:
Alexandra Silakova

Congratulations on your special little bundle of joy!

We're rooting for you and your little one! You got this!

-The Slusarenco's

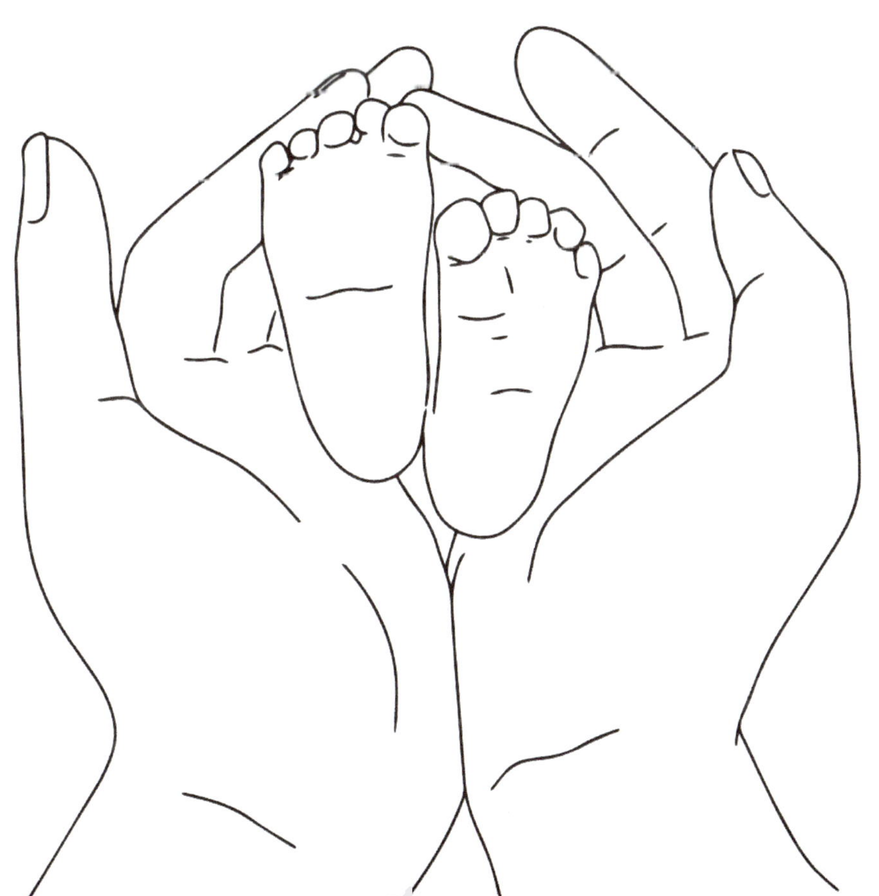

I'm a NICU baby and that's okay.

LABS

I'll get stronger every day.

It might seem hard,
some days are rough. . .

but we'll get through this,
you know I'm tough.

Don't feel bad, you did nothing wrong.

We're in this together,
let's stay strong.

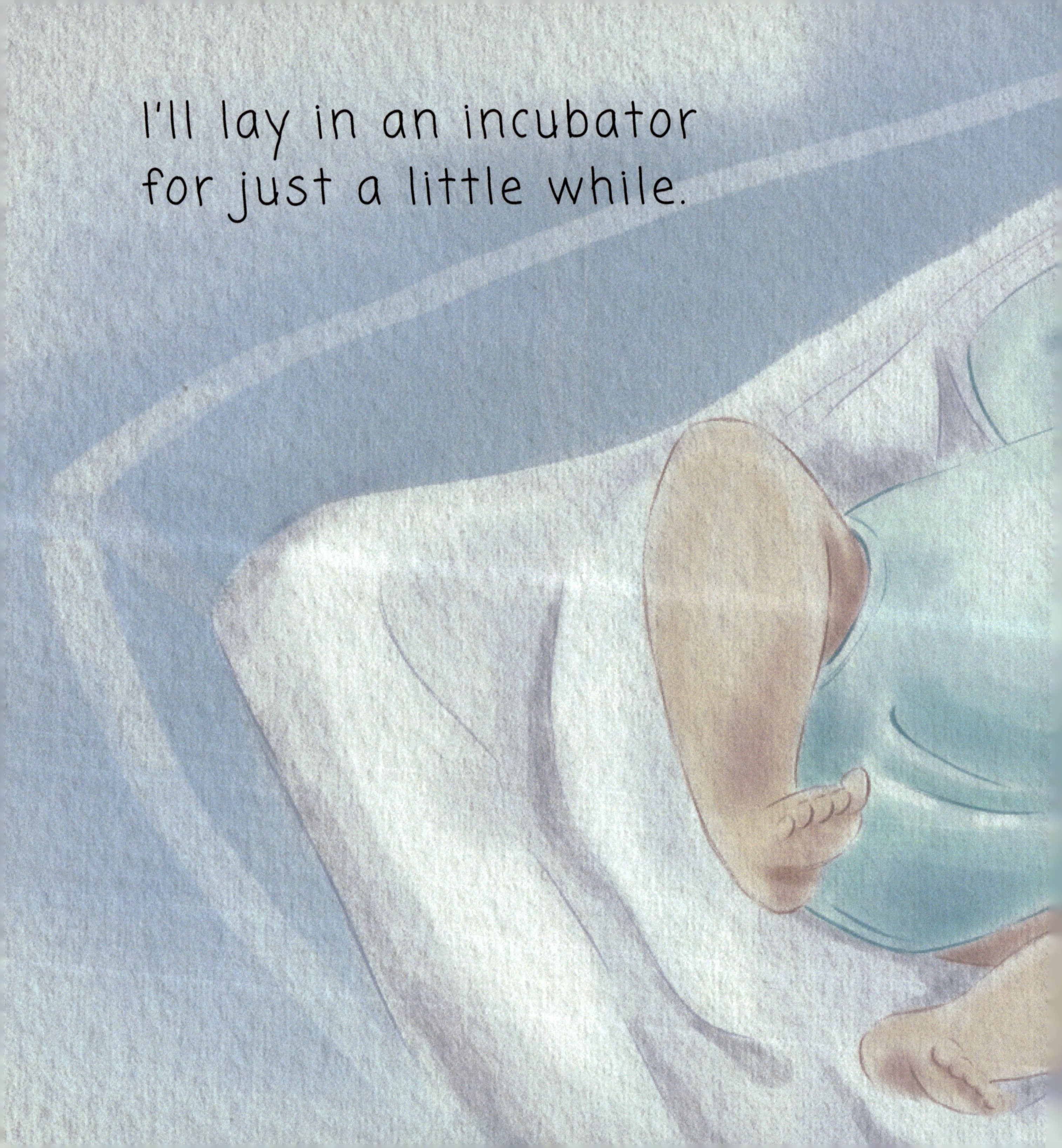

I'll lay in an incubator
for just a little while.

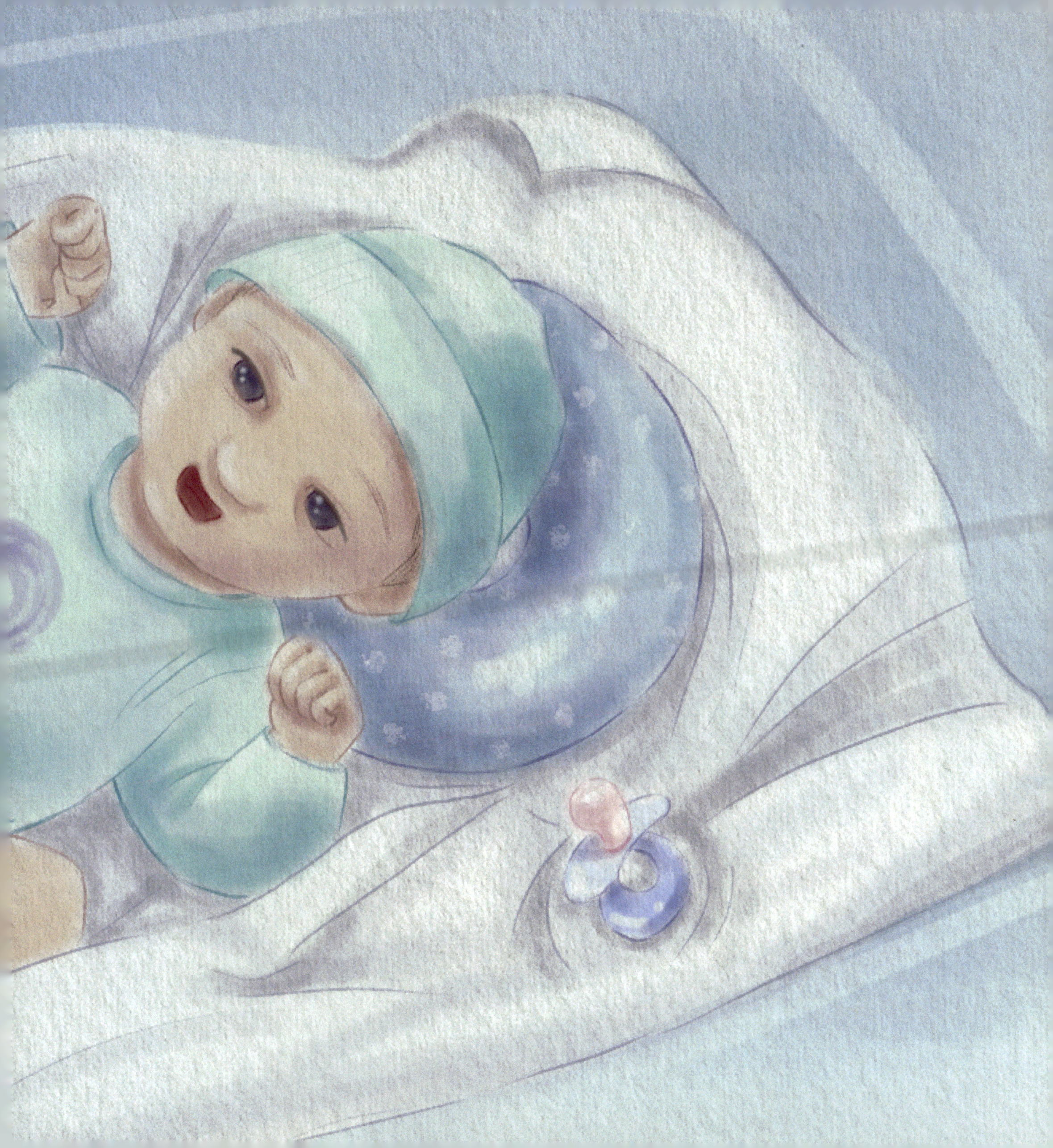

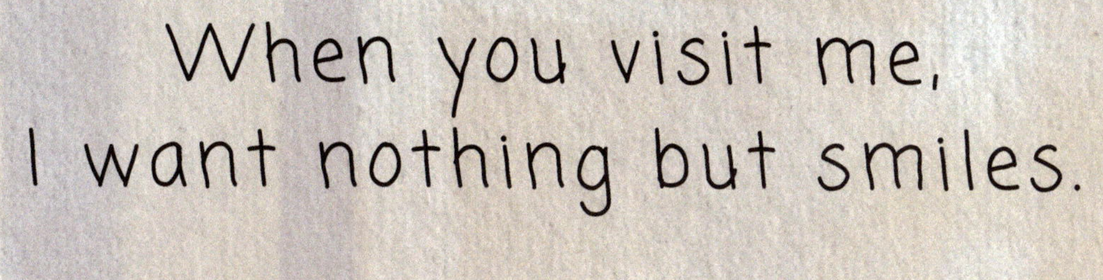

When you visit me,
I want nothing but smiles.

We're not alone,
there are others here. . .

in the best environment with
people who care.

I love when you bring me
teddy bears and toys.

BABY
OIL

When you read to me
I feel the most joy.

When my time here is
finally done. . .

we'll go home and have
so much fun!

Special Thanks!:

To the wonderful healthcare professionals who care for NICU babies and their families daily, and to our local hospital for taking great care of our twin girls while they were in the NICU. Because of you, our babies are healthy and thriving, and for that we are grateful.

Follow us!:

My twin girls were born at 29 weeks gestation. They spent around 11 weeks in the NICU after birth. We would love to share pictures and stories from our NICU journey with you! We also want to know about your experience! Find me on my 'all things NICU' Instagram:

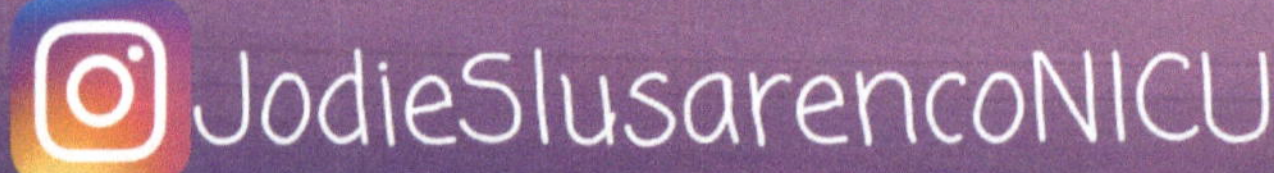